THE JOY OF HEAVEN 6

Visit to Earth and the Encounter with the Dragon

I0167845

Daniel Leske

.".…they shall MOUNT up with wings as eagles…" Isaiah 40:31

Daniel Leske

The Joy of Heaven 6: Visit to Earth and the Encounter with the Dragon by Daniel Leske
Copyright © 2019 by Daniel Leske
All Rights Reserved.
ISBN: 978-1-59755-565-4

Published by: ADVANTAGE BOOKS™
Longwood, Florida, USA
www.advbookstore.com

Library of Congress Catalog Number: 2019957985

First Printing: January 2020
20 21 22 23 24 25 26   10 9 8 7 6 5 4 3 2 1
Printed in the United States of America

Prelude

In the Joy of Heaven 6, the action of the series picks up with angels going to earth with a reason.

A note about Lucifer, in this book as the dragon. First of all, the dragon is Lucifer's armor at full strength! It's when he has the most power!

Lucifer was the most intelligent being ever created by Lord God. While he was in heaven, he was allowed to walk on .... and given this by God.

Once Lucifer and the other angels were forced out of heaven to earth, God never took this intelligence or special gifts from him. Lucifer still has this in his character, except he is evil!

Lord God vowed he would NEVER allow another archangel, elder, angel, or saint to be a part of what he did for Lucifer.

Now, book 6 is about a visit to earth. There is a season, as stated in the Bible, where the earth becomes under the power and control of Lucifer like never before known to mankind.

Not much has been written on this. This book covers a visit, yet time progresses with events on earth leading up to The Joy of Heaven 7.

DANIEL

Daniel Leske

List of Characters

Wee Angel:	She has white hair and is always a little smaller than any other angels.
Felicia:	She is about 8 or 9 years old in stature with blonde hair.
Angel Gabriella:	Angel Daniella and Angel Gabriella are identical twin angels.
Angel Daniella:	Angel Daniella and Angel Gabriella are identical twin angels.
Sir William	(Revelation) A very SPECIAL white winged horse.
Tuddley Teddy:	Animal friend to many in heaven.
Annie	Animal friend to many in heaven.
Toby	Animal friend to many in heaven.
Angel Gabrielson:	A powerful angel and messenger for the Lord Jesus. Joshua, David, and Jesus have a very important meeting with them.
Simon Peter	An apostle.

Also, the nine power angels that are a part of the mission, angels, archangels, saints, that all are a part of heaven.

In book 6, Wee Angel and Felicia continue to journey, yet a very powerful angel, Angel Gabrielson takes them as well as nine other angels on a mission to earth. Angel Gabrielson warns the dragon(Lucifer) that Lord God Almighty has numbered his time before heaven's army comes for him and those with him. The trip becomes a little warmer than expected as more of Lucifer's army starts to show, including Jezebel, the queen of Hell. The tension steps up in this book as time and prophecy of the word are coming closer together!

Daniel Leske

Chapter 1

The Joy of Heaven is Special

Most of God's little ones had left as Wee Angel, and Felicia continued to walk on the golden road away from God's Holy City. Angel Daniella and Angel Gabriella had flown away and said they would see them in heaven's time.

Tuddley Teddy, Annie, and Toby were still with them as they whistled and sang glories to the Father from their little heavenly hearts. A few birds flew by them. Then some angels in flight came near to them, and they were singing heavenly glories to the Father. Heaven was beautiful, and the moment was special as Tuddley Teddy put his head close to Felicia and Wee Angel for a big hug as he wiggled all over!

Glories from the Holy City streamed above and around them. Love was everywhere, this love that the Creator had in heaven as he said in his word. Wee Angel and Felicia smiled, laughed some more, and played with Annie, Toby, and Tuddley Teddy.

Wee Angel looked at Felicia and said, "My Felicia! Everything is so special, and the Lord has made everything so special for you since you came to heaven."

"I know that, Wee Angel!" said Felicia, "I know that!"

Felicia stood as a couple of tears came to her eyes.

"Jesus has been so good to us." she continued as Toby shook his head up and down in agreement.

Annie stood and nudged both as well!

More glories streamed in the sky past them. The heavens showed the glories as Jesus had spoken during the service. Wee Angel and Felicia talked about this as they continued to walk on!

Revelation was grazing a distance away but now flew towards them.

"Oh, he is beautiful!" Wee Angel said.

"Yes, beautiful! Beautiful! Beautiful!" added Felicia.

He landed just behind them and then walked closer until each was able to hug him as he nodded his head. There were some beautiful flowers there, and of course, Wee Angel and Felicia flew and picked a couple to put into his hair and his mane. Revelation stood and loved every minute of attention. Tuddley Teddy, Toby, and Annie were so happy as he looked at them and whinnied a mighty sound.

They played, laid on the heavenly grass, and walked over to a little stream where some ducks were swimming and quacking to each other.

Then a couple of angels came flying from the Holy city towards them, landed, introduced themselves as Angel Nathaniel, and Angel Malachi.

Wee Angel and Felicia greeted them. They were messengers from the throne. They said to Wee Angel that she was to continue to take Felicia to more heavenly places and mansions. They told Wee Angel a few of them. They said prayers with Wee Angel and Felicia and soon were in flight back to God's Holy City.

Wee Angel said, "My! My! Felicia, we are to continue to see some more special places. I will tell you more as we go there. Revelation will go with us!"

Let's take some time and rest with our friends here by the stream's edge, and then we will go to them. All of them rested a short time.

Soon they said good days to Tuddley Teddy. He stood and watched as Wee Angel and Felicia got on the back of Revelation.

Soon he opened his mighty wings, and immediately they were just above Tuddley Teddy with Toby and Annie in flight next to them. Wee Angel had Revelation make some circles in flight around Tuddley as they waved to him again and again!

Glories streamed mightily from God's Holy City, which wasn't that far away from them. Mighty glories above, upward on God's Holy mountain as they viewed it within the city.

Higher and higher Revelation flew until Tuddley was at a distance as they were going to see more of God's heaven. Joy was in their hearts.

Daniel Leske

Chapter 2

Talking about Everything

Sir William flew quietly, onward above the lands of heaven. To their surprise, his beauty was magnificent to their eyes. He would nod and look back at Wee Angel and Felicia as he flew along, then flew through a valley with trees that were glowing with various colors from their heavenly leaves. The beauty streamed above just enough to be a blessing to their beauty.

Wee Angel said, "We are going to another special prayer area. Just know it has a special beauty as all of the Lord's prayer areas do!"

"Thank you, Wee Angel!" answered Felicia. "Thank you!"

Wee Angel sat closest to Sir William's mane with Felicia sitting right behind her. Toby and Annie flew just a little behind Sir William, one to each side.

Then some angels flew upward from an area of trees and joined in with the flight. A couple of saints with wings also joined in with the quiet flight. The valley was vast with more streams, flowers, a flock of geese flew in the distance, some deer were grazing, more flowered areas, and golden paths, and an even wider golden pathway as well!

They flew just above the heavenly land, saw riders on horses, and those areas where many had places to sit for conversations, as they went about in a heavenly way. Beauty to their eyes as they had so much to reflect on in their hearts.

Both enjoyed so much as Sir William flew onward! Above them, more glories of heaven streamed, below them the beauties of the colors that covered his heavenly land that seemingly was placed perfectly there by the Father, the Creator for the saints and angels to enjoy!

They flew a little faster as Annie and Toby flew up closer to them. They looked to Sir William to say "Hi!" in their own ways as a cougar and dog would in a heavenly way.

The angels and saints continued to fly a short distance behind them as they flew closer and closer to an area that had waterfalls that cascaded from the bluffs of the mountains. Soon Sir William flew lower and closer to a group of cedar trees, with flowers that encircled them. They landed on a golden path by the trees.

The angels and saints flew onward further up the path and close to the prayer area. Soon they stood and just enjoyed the moments with much love in their hearts. They knew that the Lord had special plans for them as they talked together over everything they had seen and the glorious service, and also the roses.

"Jesus gave us each a rose, Wee Angel," said Felicia.

"Yes!" answered Wee Angel. "That was so special. I can't put into words how special that was Felicia."

"That's right!" added Felicia as more tears came to her eyes.

They knew the beauty and love in their hearts as Sir William, Toby, and Annie nodded in agreement to them. They rested by the cedar trees, then slowly walked on the golden way closer to the prayer area.

There were small waterfalls to their sides, and ahead they could see the high waterfalls. There were some bushes with fruits and berries alongside them. Within heaven's time, they came to a special rose arbor with glories and angels hovered in and around the tall hedges with large beautiful flowers on their stems.

They heard singing by the angels from the heavenly grounds. They heard some triumphant sounds too. They heard praises to the Father. Then they heard shouts of joy from the saints and angels that were present there.

"Isn't the Lord wonderful?" asked Felicia.

"Yes!" humbly answered Wee Angel.

They strolled along the stream, hearing praises, yet they talked more about Jesus, the flight, Angel Gabriella, Angel Daniella, and what had all happened to them. They felt so much in their hearts and had to share their feelings with Annie, Toby, and Sir William too! They felt the Joy of Heaven!

Chapter 3

Praises Continue

Both knew that the Lord was being so special to them and was doing so much for them. They loved the attention they got, and both were so humbled Jesus would take his time for Angel Gabriella, Angel Daniella, and them.

"Oh, look at the roses!" added Felicia as saints flew, and saints walked past them on the golden way into the prayer area.

They soon took Sir William, Toby, Annie, to a grazing area for them to wait and rest by a group of trees like the palm trees on earth with a large fruit tree close by them. Both walked through the hedges into the beautiful prayer area where the Saints were in prayer with other angels. The falls cascaded into streams a short distance from where they were.

The prayer area was the base with falls of water that came from bluffs to their sides. Hedges and streams below, along the sides, and above the hedges, angels hovered in flight, singing choruses of heavenly sounds. Some had instruments, and others hovered with hallelujahs and praises that came forth for the saints and angels in prayer.

"Some of the sounds," whispered Wee Angel, "are so they can reach the depths of our heavenly soul!"

Felicia said, "I have never heard sounds like these before! My heart is already so stirred, and now this. Oh, the love that I feel in my heart!"

"That is what they are for Felicia," answered Wee Angel, "to touch our heavenly soul as the light does for us. It's heaven's way, and we are a part of this."

They listened to the heavenly sounds that these special angels voiced to everyone who was there. They spent some time in prayer and praise, as they thanked the Lord for His beautiful ways. They prayed for earth and remembered the flight that they had with the Lord and his army. They just knew to pray about this.

There were rows of benches and places to sit for the saints and angels. These were to the sides by the streams with small bushes present, special flowered areas, and some smaller trees. The area was wide, yet not vast.

The waterfalls and the sounds from these special angels were beautiful. They hovered around and above the hedges in between the prayer areas and the falls.

They soon left through the archway of special flowers, more angels, with glories all above the area in the heavenly sky. They soon were back with Toby, Sir William, and Annie. They took some time to play and talk to them and to let them know how much they loved them.

Some saints came and talked to them. There was Michael, Evelyn, Becky, Montgomery, Sam, Terrance, and Alex. Of course, they greeted the animals, played with them, and soon were on their way in another flight.

It was time to leave, so Wee Angel and Felicia were on Sir William's back and soon were in flight going higher and higher over the high bluffs, then along the top of the ridge of flat-like mountains which had many streams that flowed from the distance on top of this range.

Sir William nodded to what Wee Angel whispered to him. Wee Angel said to Toby and Annie that they should fly to the heavenly lands and that they would see them again in heavenly time. With this Annie and Toby flew very close to Sir William, Wee Angel, and Felicia and seemingly smiled in their way, wiggled a little, nodded their heads a little, and then flew away and lower from them as Sir William started to fly higher and higher to their destination in heaven.

Chapter 4

Continue to Reflect

They flew onward, and then in heavens time, they came to several long winding wide pathways with trees to both sides with high billowy clouds with many glories, up and away from them.

Sir William flew towards an area with trees around a massive rock formation with other spires of rocks. The scene was very majestic. There were glories all around, with majestic trees that grew in and around the many rock formations. There were canyons to the sides, and the wide pathways were paved with the finest gold.

By the rocks were beautiful streams and more waterfalls. These falls cascaded through the rocks, and then they wound through the canyons that were beside the pathways that wound between and along the canyons. These pathways went as far as their heavenly eyes could see with glories of light streaming in the distance that came from God's Holy City.

The sky was so beautiful as Sir William winged towards an open area along one of the wide pathways. Trees encircled the area where he landed softly on some grass. There were beautiful tall pine trees with very dark greens. The fragrance was so awesome, with pinecones so big even to their heavenly eyes.

Again, light streamed from the trees as there were no shadows in heaven, only light, no gray areas. Just beautiful light out and about everything that God created, even the rocks had a golden hue emanating from them. There were no dull colors as on earth.

Wee Angel and Felicia sat by the edge of a stream. They took turns to go into the stream and splashed water, played and just were happy! They continued to reflect on what Felicia saw as they passed over heaven's lands.

Above them, many geese flew, and a gentle breeze was there.

Wee Angel said, "Remember when I met you amongst the lilies."

Every now and then, Wee Angel and Felicia talked of their first meeting in heaven. Of course, Wee Angel would always say how she saw Felicia and even Daniel on earth. She would tell Felicia about Daniel, and of course, both talked and wondered how he was doing!"

"God always tells me He is doing fine, and I'm keeping him busy. That's all Lord God says to me when I see him at the throne room," said Wee Angel.

"Yes, I'm glad you shared that with me, Wee Angel," said Felicia. "We will keep praying for him till we see him here."

"Yes, Felicia, that's right!" added Wee Angel.

Sir William nodded a big nod to them, and then he whinnied a mighty sound to the heavenly sky as if he knew something special about Daniel."

Then Wee Angel and Felicia hugged Sir William, and they continued to talk and reflect on everything. Above, many angels flew in both directions, coming and going to their destinations. Some saints rode past them on horses. These had no wings but were very beautiful in stature.

The saints waved, smiled, and showed the glories of heavenly life in their faces.

"Oh, what joy in their faces." continued Felicia. "Isn't it something how every saint, angel, has such a beautiful countenance here in heaven," added Wee Angel. "It's so special, as on earth!"

Both took time and prayed for the life on earth and the ways of the Lord would be there and will be as he promised by his Word.

They thanked the Lord and again felt so much joy in their hearts.

Chapter 5

Waiting for Something Special

They knew the Lord was showing them and sharing with them His ways and His concern for the earth. Soon Sir William with both on his back, opened up his mighty wings and he was in heaven's skies. He flew just along and above the winding wide golden way.

They continued to fly over saints, and saints on horses that traveled on the golden road that had several rows of trees to the sides that were perfectly spaced and as well flowers about each tree. Beautiful stones to the sides of the wide golden pathway.

They could see the canyons to the sides. Yet, at the top side of the canyons, a hedge went all along the edge so saints could look over the hedge at the beauty of the canyons that had many waterfalls, streams, rock formations, streams of light from prayer areas in the distances.

Sir William flew over, and soon they flew past another prayer area between the golden roads. They saw the saints in prayer as they were to fly around this area and not directly over it. They saw the angels along and above the golden ways. Sir William flew higher and higher into heaven's skies to another place in heaven.

Both were now relaxed and viewed the wonderful lands of heaven. Their hearts were full of so much love and emotions. They knew so much!

Wee Angel saw an area of beautiful bushes along the golden pathway that still was high on the top side of these mountains.

Sir William landed by the most beautiful flowering bushes, trees with several streams, and small waterfalls.

The area was so quietly beautiful with many orchid flowers along the wide pathway, several palm-like trees with special tall evergreen trees up and along some small hills. Each knew they were in the presence of the Lord. They knew something or someone from the throne was going to be there.

Wee Angel knew this, and Felicia sensed this as they now walked about and looked at everything close to them.

They sat, groomed Sir William, flew some circles up and around the trees, ate some berries that were close to them, looked at the small waterfalls, ran a little, and then sat again under one of the trees. They just knew that they were to wait there for someone from the throne of the Lord's.

They sat quietly and talked, had fellowship, prayed, thanked the Lord for everything.

Within heaven's time, both looked to the horizon from God's Holy City, and then they saw why they were waiting there. Along and coming closer to them were several mighty angels of the Lord. They knew this by the tremendous light that surrounded and went from them as they flew closer to them. It was like all light, yet both just knew there was more than one angel.

Both were excited in their hearts as they watched them come closer and closer.

Chapter 6

Specialness becomes the Mission

Soon the angels were close enough to see them. There were ten mighty angels that the Lord used for special missions and trips to earth to protect and fulfill his plans! Their power is less than the archangels, yet they still were extremely powerful compared to other angels in heaven like Wee Angel and saints.

They gently flew just above Wee Angel, Felicia and Sir William, then all landed close to them. The leader of this angel grouping was Angel Gabrielson. He was a lot like Gabriel in stature and power. He spoke to Wee Angel and Felicia, telling them that they would be guided on a special journey to earth.

He said, "We should leave Sir William here for now as the ruling of the Lord is that there be no winged horses on earth until He takes them there as the Bible reads! So Sir William will wait right here and graze. There will be other horses coming by here as well as little friends."

Gabrielson continued, "Now both of you will be alright as we will be going fast and quickly! You will be within the mighty power of light that the Lord has given to us. There is a reason why you are being guided on this trip."

Wee Angel and Felicia hugged Sir William telling him to stay and wait there. They soon were ready for the journey.

Soon they were up into heaven's skies with all light around them. Felicia and Wee Angel could still see heaven's land, but within heaven's time, they flew higher and further away from heaven's lands. Then this light and flight of these angels quicken mightily for Wee Angel, and Felicia saw only the light as they traveled quickly with these mighty angels.

Onward! Onward! Onward this light flashed through the heavens towards the earth.

Onward! Onward! Onward! This powerful light with the angels, Felicia, and Wee Angel flashed through heaven's space towards the earth. Onward, the light flashed quickly! The light, their power, flashed quickly! It flashed because that is all anyone on earth would see as the light passed them.

In God's eyes, this flash of this light contained mighty power if and ever needed for helping those in trouble during storms, or even warfare on earth. This is God's way of protecting his own on earth and keeping order to everything as he was still the commander-in-chief of the universe, no matter what the thoughts of mankind might say!

Onward they flashed at high speeds, and soon they were close to the earth, and then they slowed down as they arrived on earth. Wee Angel and Felicia finally could smile after the journey.

Chapter 7

Showing Them the Dragon

They were above the waters of one of the oceans on earth. Here they slowed so they could rest after the long flight as they had traveled a long distance. It was here that Angel Gabrielson said to Wee Angel and Felicia that they were going to show them a little about the dragon, Lucifer, and his ways upon the earth.

Angel Gabrielson did not say too much. But he did say that we came here for a specific reason.

With this the angels proceeded more and more over the waters of the ocean.

They knew where to go to find the dragon that the Lord had cast down to earth. They knew where he was at the moment, so they flew onward! Now they flew very slowly as compared to coming to earth. Wee Angel, Felicia, Angel Gabrielson, and the other angels viewed the billowy clouds, the sunshine, the waves of the waters of the ocean.

They were getting closer to the country which Jesus formed and started that he talked about in the Bible, the United States of America. They knew the turmoil that had come to this land and its changes that were not pleasing to the Lord as more ways and laws had torn them further from His way. The Lord's way for families is to have a protected good life on earth during their life season.

The angels knew there was a warfare coming against the dragon, the fallen angels of God, yet they knew this was not the time! Lord God, Jesus and the Holy Spirit said to find the dragon and watch him for a short time.

Onward they flew as they headed closer to the dragon. Wee Angel knew some about him.

Angels that would come and go to earth are hedged in by the power of the Lord so that they only see what is necessary, not knowing what the dragon is doing on earth.

Soon they could see the swirling of the sky with their heavenly eyes as they could see what the earthly eyes of mankind could not see in the spiritual warfare. They could see the swirls formed as the dragon went about his evil ways.

The skies churned by his presence because of his extreme power. They saw blackness, and streaks of pitch blackness almost like tar in the skies.

They flew onward as Angel Gabrielson flew close to Wee Angel and Felicia.

He said, "Both of you will be very safe. Just know that is why there are ten angels to make sure you are safe."

Wee Angel said, "Thank you, Angel Gabrielson as Felicia and I were wondering about that!"

Angel Gabrielson continued, "This is not the first time that angels like us have come to watch the enemy of earth and us. The dragon knows this because he also knows his season is getting short."

Wee Angel nodded in agreement as they did understand, so with this, the three prayed for the Lord's protection over them.

They flew on closer to where the dragon would be at that time.

Chapter 8

First Meeting with the Dragon

Above the land, they saw the flashing of fire through the skies. They knew he was at an important city of the country, and they knew the dragon was stirring the fires of turmoil in the air with hatred and pride, as well as other issues talked about in the Lord's Word.

Those that are protected by the Spirit of the Lord sense little, but those that give way to his way sense and carry out acts not being right and at times, evil.

They saw the dragon swoop across part of the city with fire going everywhere. They saw that the motion of him as one head to the dragon, but as the head moved, they saw seven heads with necks circling the body of the dragon in a swift, yet very jerky manner. His tail would whip at mighty speeds with his reddish, blood-like scaly body. Trails of blackness and clouds followed him.

He was not pretty to look at as God had made him, but there was a wonderment in his appearance!

The ten angels were close and around Felicia and Wee Angel. There was tremendous power around them as they flew under the protection of the Spirit of God.

The dragon spotted them on the horizon, so in an instant of time, he was very close to them. Great cursing came from his mouth, as he roared past the powerful angels, with waves of fire that went past them.

Wee Angel and Felicia saw snakes in flight, others clinging to the dragon's body. Both held onto their riders tighter and tighter! They looked at forms of snakes, serpents with demonic faces of men and women in demonic form as the dragon flew towards, above, and circling the angels. They would appear in the clouds of darkness and then be gone!

The fire from his nostrils emitted a deep black smoke that looked like hot tar. As the flames quieted, the smoke lingered!

The dragon knew that he could only go so close to them, but in many ways it did not stop him from blowing, steam, fire, and curses at them.

The skies seemed to be aflame at his presence as he was angry and ready to battle the angels of God.

Out of his mouth, he spoke, "Why are you here on my land. This is my home. Stay away from it. This is my dwelling. Go back to your kingdom. Leave me alone. Are not all these people mine? The people are my people. Leave them alone. They are mine. My souls! My souls! My Souls for my kingdom....cursing!"

On and on, the dragon spoke as he flew high above the angels that hovered in the sky over the land.

Clouds of fire billowed around him. Black light and his power were going everywhere!

Angel Gabrielson said to Wee Angel and Felicia, "Just know you are safe!"

At the moment, neither Wee Angel and Felicia were too sure!

Yet they hovered in the same area since the dragon continued to fly quickly below, then above, and all around them.

Then it happened with one great shout Angel Gabrielson shouted across the land!

The power from him flashed mightily with a strong light like the sun and lightning. It ripped around and over the dragon, shaking him in flight.

Angel Gabrielson voice ripped through the skies towards Lucifer, "The elders, Lord God are meeting and your season on earth is now being counted many days, and we will be coming for you and your fallen angels, and your army! IT WILL BE DONE!"

The dragon at that moment laughed and then cursed on and on!

The ten angels knew it was now time to go! They came to deliver the message to Lucifer, the dragon, and now they slowly flew away from the area.

Chapter 9

The Dragon is Very Angry

As they flew the dragon, still flew quickly by them with great shock waves to them in flight, billowed clouds of smoke, fire, the cursing continued from his mouth as he shouted, "This earth is mine. I will prevail! These souls are mine! Mine! Mine!"

With this Angel Gabrielson spoke to his angels, Wee Angel and Felicia, as they quietly flew onward with great power all around them. The dragon knew that, yet both sides knew the time for battle was yet to come!

The dragon flew quickly downward, like the speed of high winds, he flew!

Trees ripped from their roots and debris was flying everywhere with waters from a nearby river exploding upwards as he flung his trail and pushed more and more waters upward.

Boats and fishing boats with passengers were hurled upwards like a tornado had hit them! Cars flew to the sides of the road and into trees!

More trees flew and shredded upward!

A crowd of people gathered together were whipped quickly by his tail in the air as his anger grew!

A church nearby was hit and the roof shattered with glass from windows flying everywhere! More trees were ripped, shredded by his flight and his tail. He flung a person into the ground with dirt over the body! Droplets of blood on the dirt. Droplets of blood now were being left by him on branches of trees, across the land, and across the waters. Soon puddles of blood formed by trees.

Damaged houses with blood splattered on them, more bodies lay on the ground and in trees.

With his wings he hurled blood everywhere! The puddles were now more like pools of blood.

Odors of hell filled the air. Wee Angel whispered to Felicia that Jesus has the fragrance of roses and spice, while the dragon has the odor of death and rotten flesh! Black clouds of smoke were everywhere!

The dragon flew high above the group of angels ripping the air, and the clouds of fire billowed around him like a bomb with fires, light, and his power was going everywhere!

Angel Gabrielson said to Wee Angel and Felicia, "Just know you are safe!"

Yet they hovered in the same area because the anger of the dragon continued to fly all around them.

They saw the dragon in his anger over what Angel Gabrielson had said, rip through more trees and some places, dwellings, and houses on earth where debris flew everywhere.

Then Angel Gabrielson and the angels saw on the horizon other creatures from hell flying upward above the horizon to meet the dragon. They watched and saw the formations of other creatures of the dragon's kingdom, with more fallen angels present and on this massing army of the devil's.

They saw snake-like reptile-like forms rising now high above into the skies with power like the dragon. They saw hideous serpents, angelic beings, yet garbed in warlike armor that was serpent-like in looks, yet they seemed ready to fight the armies of heaven.

Also present were some of the fallen angels that were the most powerful angels that fell with Lucifer.

They had a blackness to their faces, yet still an angel-like appearance in their stature. Their armor was black with piercing red blood-like gems on their shields and breastplates. Their light was a black light with rays of blackness all about them. Such that it seemed hard to see their form, but more as a cold black light that seemed very powerful.

Wee Angel said to Felicia, "I'm sad to see these fallen angels. There is a sadness in my heart, to know they once were mighty to the Lord."

Then the sadness went away as she continued, "I'm alright now! I'm alright now! They are not the same now! They are now only evil and think evil!"

Felicia said, "I know what you are trying to say!"

They were hideous. Wee Angel and Felicia knew they had great power.

Angel Gabrielson told Wee Angel and Felicia quietly, " Lord God Almighty had made Lucifer the most powerful angel in heaven and the most intelligent being ever created either in heaven or on earth. God allowed Lucifer to do and or gave Lucifer something extraordinary, but after what happened between Him and Lucifer, Lord God the creator said he never, ever would allow another archangel, angel or elder or anyone to have, and or do to have this again. He never took this away from Lucifer when he was cast down to earth. This makes Lucifer extremely powerful. All those gifts, plus this unknown, are still with him till the battle is over! The fallen angels as well have power. This all has to be dealt with by God."

Wee Angel and Felicia nodded to Angel Gabrielson as they continued their flight. They continued to fly away slowly! They were now back over the ocean.

They saw the dragon in the far distance. They could still see the anger in his swirls with smoke and debris flying upwards. Then just like the flash of a lightning bolt, the dragon was right next to them, shouting, cursing at the group, yet he could not do anything to hurt the armor placed around them with their mighty power.

He rose high above them, shouting obscenities, then went on, "My Kingdom earth! My kingdom! These(cursing) people are mine and my army.

Then they looked at the dragon as he continued to huff with his nostrils, tremendous fires came from them. They saw the one head, yet in an instant, the head would swirl mightily and then they could see the seven heads and necks molded into one body. The seven heads would twist and turn, moving and turning on the seven necks, much like snakes as one head would come close to them and then another with flashing motion like the speed of light. Fires flew out and around the angels as these heads flashed out and around them with tremendous smoke and heat.

The angels had tremendous power so that none of it penetrated them, yet one couldn't have said that to Wee Angel or Felicia as they were hoping just to get away from there.

More fires came past them as the heads whipped and turned past and around them. Their shields of powerful light protected them, but it was affecting them in they would be moving quickly up and down, left and right from the shock and waves of power from the dragon.

Felicia and Wee Angel felt it getting very warm around them as all of them hovered and flew slowly in the best manner possible. Finally, some of the angels fired back their power of light, forcing the heads to slow and Lucifer to back off from them. The dragon did not expect this and shook a little, but then more cursing came from his mouth.

Angel Gabrielson said to them, "We did not come to fight him, but we had to finally do something to protect you from him. Just know these angels with us are very powerful too!"

With this, Felicia and Wee Angel stayed calmer in knowing these angels had tremendous power too! They looked at the ocean waters and saw them with tremendous turbulence because of everything that was occurring with waters flying upwards, waterspouts in the air and black clouds forming at the horizon. The air seemed like it was on fire.

The dragon then went flying further away from them, but then turned flew upwards and closer again to them. The top part of the body started to change before their eyes as if the forces were lifted and the armor of the dragon was taken away from him with tremendous power.

They saw it was the face of Lucifer!

The face had an angel-likeness under the surface of dragon as the body, the light went to a deep black darkness away from his angel-like body. They saw how his body as they looked molded with scale-like marks, small scales with the light showing through them. As you looked down his body of dragon with tail, one saw, how the scales started to mold into a serpent-like body, then more dragon-like as the reptiles that are present on earth.

Wee Angel said to Felicia, "God said in his word, Lucifer is a creature and how mankind would serve the creature more than the Creator. God is the Creator and his power is this and separates Him from all beings. Lucifer is like a serpent, and the dragon is his armor for protection.

They saw this powerful beast, the creature, the dragon in one body and one head. More smoke and fires flew out of his mouth right at them and around the ten angels. More curses came from his mouth.

The dragon flew further away from them towards an ever-increasing army of the dragon-like beings, that were a part of his army.

They flew onward as a powerful light force and slowly higher and higher. Angel Gabrielson was leading and guiding them onwards, slowly trying to get them further and further upward. They were still over the waters of the ocean.

Again the dragon came closer with many, but they were still at a distance. They were hissing like snakes. There was a terrible odor in the skies as snake-like patterns formed all around and the hissing, great hissing sounds, and sounds like reptiles.

Then more dragon-like lizard formed creatures with wings appeared close to the angels. All the creature like forms had riders with armor-like plates on their bodies, serpent-like armor with tremendous black flashes of light going out and away from them.

Chapter 10

Jezebel Arrives
and the
Angels are Glad to be Leaving

Wee Angel knew these riders were fallen angels as their heads and being still had an angel-like appearance, but no light, only dark light instead swirled mightily about them.

Then they saw at a distance a large lizard-flying creature like the dragon with a woman being on it. Angel Gabrielson knew who she was as he told Wee Angel and Felicia, "That is the queen of hell. That is the one as marked or quoted as Jezebel. She is second in command in hell right next to Lucifer."

Wee Angel saw a beauty in her, yet feared her presence, as her hair looked like her hair had snakes, serpent-like creatures, that encircled her being.

Snakes in flight were everywhere around her. Jezebel and a large snake-like creature were molded together with scales, and blood oozing from it. There was a pool of blood molded into the snake just in front of her.

Her face was not devil-like, but more of glamor and suggestive power as one was drawn to her face.

Felicia said, "She still looks like a woman. Her face seems to be very pretty!"

Her black hair was very drawing, long down past her neck. Her garb was somewhat revealing, but much like a robe of a queen of a kingdom. The snakes made her look scary but still drawn to her power and appearance. Tremendous power from her!

Felicia said, "My! The power from her!"

Wee Angel nodded in agreement, "She is very powerful but totally evil! She only thinks evil!"

Then in a flash, she and the creature were gone!

Even Angel Gabrielson looked at the other nine angels, Wee Angel and Felicia, in astonishment and wonder for he did not expect her to make an appearance to them. They knew then that the dragon and her were already concerned over the message they had delivered from God Almighty.

Soon all the smoke, those of the dragon's army, were gone away from them as quickly as they had come there.

Wee Angel and Felicia finally felt like they could breathe with everything that had happened to them. Yes, they knew they were safe, but again you could not have told that to them.

The group of angels flew onward, faster and faster back toward heaven. All of the angels were happy and joyful! None of them had expected the dragon's queen to be there or his army to start joining in with more power on their side.

Each flew now up by Wee Angel and Felicia and asked them, "Are you alright? Just know we did not expect to stir up so many of the dragon's army."

Felicia and Wee Angel felt better and better now that speeds inside this light force became quicker and quicker.

Onward inside the light!

Onward! Onward! Onward through heavenly space!

Soon they saw the glowing of the Holy lights of heaven. The heaven where God's Holy City is located!

They flashed onward, soon slowing and seeing heaven's lands, back near the very place they had left in heaven.

Wee Angel hugged Angel Gabrielson for a long time. They said, "We are so glad to be back and safe here."

Then they hugged the other nine angels too! They walked and talked with the ten angels for a long heavenly time getting their little heavenly hearts calm! The angels wanted to make sure everything was alright with them.

Then they found Sir William grazing by some trees. All of them had prayer, thanked the Lord for their safe journey and his protection. Within heaven's time, Angel Gabrielson flew upwards with the other angels as they headed back to God's Holy City to see Jesus at the Throne Room.

Chapter 11

Back and Safe

Wee Angel and Felicia walked towards Sir William, and as they walked, they spotted a little deer with him.

Wee Angel knew the little deer as Little Angelica. Felicia was there, and both greeted Sir William and the two animals. The little deer had spots and also wings. Oh, she was so pretty. More hugs!

Wee Angel said, "Felicia, most deer in heaven run free like those on earth with no wings. The Lord said they were made to run and be free to run as on earth. The deer like it that way! Some have wings, and Little Angelica is one of them."

They took a lot of time to play and be with Sir William and Little Angelica. Both Wee Angel and Felicia talked about the visit to earth with the angels. Again they were delighted to be back on heaven's lands after this.

They knew that they were protected, yet that did not take away any of the emotions they felt being surrounded by one furious and mighty dragon. The buildup of his army of fallen angels and creatures that neither Felicia or Wee Angel liked that existed in some places on earth. They were glad they were there and not in heaven.

Soon Sir William almost demanded more attention from Wee Angel and Felicia, for they knew that he had missed them. Each flew and found a beautiful heavenly flower, much like the dahlia's on earth, and placed a couple in his mane.

Within heaven's time, they were ready to leave the area when Felicia looked to the distance and saw a couple of angels flying towards them. Soon they saw that it was Angel Gabriella and Angel Daniella. Everyone greeted everyone, and of course, Wee Angel and Felicia shared with them the experience they just had in going to earth.

"My! My! My! My! My!" both Angel Daniella and Angel Gabriella kept saying together.

"Are you alright?" Angel Daniella asked them.

"Yes! Yes! Maybe!" they answered quietly, trying to find words as these came out of them.

Angel Gabriella said, "We were told that we should go to a praise service from here."

They told Wee Angel where it was, so she instructed Sir William, and soon all were into the heavenly skies with Little Angelica flying right along with them.

They viewed beautiful forests of trees as they flew along just above them. Their flight was about as slow as they could go, for they just wanted to enjoy and be thankful for everything that they saw because of the journey.

Wee Angel flew around some trunks of the trees with Angel Daniella and Angel Gabriella following while Felicia stayed on the back of Sir William. Now they were relaxed and felt the love and joy of heaven again in their hearts.

Small rivers flowed outward and away from the forest of trees. Higher mountains to the left of them and as they flew along, there were some vast open waters to their right like our seas on earth.

They continued to fly slowly, enjoying the beauty of heaven. In heaven's time, they saw some more tall mountains ahead of them with more tall trees and waterfalls. They saw a huge gate-like entrance between the bluffs of the mountains. There was a pasture area near the gate, and this was where Sir William landed gently on the grass.

They continued to talk and share, while Sir William and Little Angelica started to graze by a stream. They left Sir William and Little Angelica there as they walked to the gate of beautiful geraniums with vines that went high upward and little falls of water that slowly fell from high above from the bluffs of the mountain.

All laughed and even giggled over the beauty and love they felt in their hearts. They greeted other saints and angels that came on a golden path towards the flowered gate or entrance.

There were other horses and animals in the pasture, which included some sheep, more deer, and antelope.

Chapter 12

A Beautiful Service

They walked in through the entrance and into a beautiful yet smaller sanctuary. It had trees along the sides, with the bluffs of the mountains going straight up, covered with flowers.

The flowers were grouped and made the mountainside look like a quilt with the different groupings of flowers of the same color yet had many colors to make up the walls of the sanctuary.

There were small waterfalls, where the water fell down from streams on top of the bluffs and places where the waterfalls were formed by water coming through the openings in the mountainside. They created beautiful streams along the sides of the sanctuary.

All of them found a place to sit and they looked with awe at all the beauty. Other saints and angels were there too.

Many little angels started to fly around along the bluffs. Hundreds of Little angels as Wee Angel looked with fine eyes and again she noticed that all of them were just a little bit taller than her.

Wee Angel said to Felicia, "They are all taller than me!"

Felicia smiled and said to Wee Angel, "You know Wee Angel, I wouldn't want it any other way. I am so thankful you are the size you are!"

Both Angel Gabriella and Angel Daniella agreed as they comforted Wee Angel. The small angels sang! Some had instruments. What a beautiful moment, hearing their voices and the beautiful music they sang as they praised the heavenly Father.

"It's so glorious," said Angel Gabriella.

It was a smaller worship, yet the beauty was awesome! After it was over, the little angels came one by one, by one to them and introduced themselves.

"I'm Angel Sherry!"

"I'm Angel Holly!"

"I'm Angel Ernie!

"I'm Angel Penny!"

"I'm Angel Ben!"

"I'm Angel Clover!"

"I'm Angel Nate!"

"I'm Angel Hannah!

On and on they came to them and introduced themselves.

They said, "We have heard so much about you. Thank you!"

More little angels came up to them.

"I'm Angel Rose!

"I'm Angel Lite!

"I'm Angel Will!

It continued! A beautiful moment as the four again had tears in their eyes as all these little angels greeted them.

Within time, they were outside the entrance, walking, talking, being thankful over the beauty, and all their little friends. With Sir William were two more little friends. On his back were two large crane-like birds. They were Crown and Halo! So, they flew over to Angel Gabriella and Angel Daniella for a little attention.

Soon all of them walked along on the golden path through trees along the mountains.

In time they came to a court area for saints and angels. Here the four found places to sit, visit, and rest! Beautiful steps of waterfalls went through the trees over beautiful stones that had light coming through them. Gems were placed just right in the courtyard with beautiful golden gems in short columns or pillar-like, around a circular area with the bushes and trees spaced evenly apart from one another.

Within heavens' time, Angel Gabriella and Angel Daniella said, "We must be going again!"

So again, hugs and good days were given to all the little ones, including Sir William.

"We will find you again!" said Angel Daniella.

They all smiled for they were close friends. Away they flew!

"It's hard to see them fly away," said Felicia, "but I know here in heaven, we will always see them again!"

With a big smile on her face, Wee Angel said, "That's right, Felicia!"

Sir William had whinnied in agreement. He felt the same as them.

Daniel Leske

Chapter 13

Happy to Be Back with Friends

Crown and Halo stood quietly on the back of Sir William. They loved every second of being there and the attention they received from both Wee Angel and Felicia.

They were happy and loved this moment in heaven, as each loved the Father in the ways a bird, a horse, a deer, an angel, and now Felicia could love the Father.

In time after much talk, Wee Angel said, "We are going to continue walking, then there is an opening amongst the trees so that Sir William can start to fly!"

"I'm ready again!" added Felicia. "I'm so happy inside. I love everything so much, and I am so thankful, Wee Angel. I have you and Sir William as friends, and we have met so many friends."

With this, Little Angelica came quietly by Felicia and put her little head close by hers. She nudged Felicia for a hug.

Felicia hugged her little neck so tightly, "My little one, Angelica! You are so sweet and beautiful!"

Now Wee Angel and Felicia had a few tears again! Tears of joy from all that had happened to them. They had been to many places in heaven, including God's Holy City, and the throne room.

They talked awhile, yet all of them walked past some beautiful forest trees, as they ate some fruit while they walked and continued along the golden path, through the forest. Soon they were on Sir William's back, and with his mighty wings, he flew upward above the trees with Crown, Halo, and Little Angelica flying right behind him.

They flew above the forest with a mountain to their side. Then Sir William started to fly more upward to their next destination in heaven. A beautiful sight, as he flew across, above more streams, golden paths, saints, angels in flight, just above heaven's lands.

The sight was awesome as the life in heaven is beautiful with the glories of God's skies showing his love for those that love him in their new home as he, being the Creator, did for them for eternity. Now in heaven's time, they kept flying, but then oft in the distance, they saw a very brilliant light and the light was coming slowly closer!

Soon, Wee Angel and Felicia saw, it was the power riders on their white-winged horses. The leader of this group came closer and closer to Sir William. Soon he motioned to them that they should follow them. He said his name was Galihad, while Wee Angel nodded, and Sir William knew!

With this, Sir William flew in behind the winged horses and followed them. They flew onward as the light from this group was always very strong and powerful to the eyes. They soon started to fly higher and faster above heaven's lands. Then they flew upward into heaven's skies. Onward they flew, and as they flew, there was a huge light stream going upward away from heaven's land.

In a short time, the group of winged horses with Sir William were in the light stream. Crown and Halo stood on the back of Sir William, just behind Wee Angel and Felicia. Little Angelica flew very close and right next to Sir William.

Upward, the group flew into this powerful light to a special place or mansion in heaven.

Chapter 14

A Special Place for Winged Horses and Riders

Within heaven's time, they started to see glimpses of their destination as they flew through a very wide gate or archway into the skies of this special mansion. Once in the skies of the mansion, they saw pastures below them with many beautiful white-winged horses. These horses grazed, and there were some little hills about the area with small mountains in the distance.

Around the sides of the wide pasture were courtyards of beautiful gems, stones, waterfalls, special areas of flowers, trees, with golden paths. It was like a huge valley with courtyards all around the sides of the pastures. Many small courtyards, yet what a beautiful sight. There were dwellings made of gems and fine gold in amongst the hills that surrounded the pastures. The dwellings were for the power riders.

They flew above and soon landed near one of the courtyards. Small waterfalls, with many steps, fountains of water, beautiful flowers, the grass streamed with light as did all the trees, shrubs in this mansion.

Beautiful colors to their eyes. They saw other riders walking and taking care of the horses. Even in heaven, the Lord had these riders taking care of these white horses. Galihad talked with Wee Angel and Felicia. Then he bid them good days as he went his way.

Soon an angel walked along a golden path towards them. His name was Angel Psalms.

He said, "Wee Angel, Felicia, take a little time for rest, walk about here, and then we will be flying you back to heaven's lands!"

So they talked with Angel Psalms, made sure Little Angelica was alright, and Sir William was busy grazing with some other horses.

Soon in heaven's time, Angel Psalms said, "Let's head back, the Lord wanted you to see a small part of where his horses and riders lived here." Soon they flew back into the archway of light that was above this mansion, and all of them flew onward back to heaven's land. They flew onward and landed in a special place of flowers, meadows, with many little ones about such as geese, ducks, deer, and other animals of heaven.

Angel Psalms bid them a good day, and he was soon in flight to another place in heaven.

Wee Angel and Felicia found some fruit and then rested by some beautiful shrubs by a stream. As they sat, a few saints came up to them. Their names were Alan, Jim, Bonnie, Melody, Allison, Dawn, and Linda. They talked, then they formed a circle and held hands and prayed.

Wee Angel prayed, "Thank you, Jesus, for these saints. Thank you, Lord, for the beautiful moments that I've been able to share with Felicia. Thank you for Sir William, Little Angelica, and your little ones. Thank you, Lord, for all the angels we have met! Thank you, Lord! All of us, praise, and we love you, Lord."

Soon the saints went on their way. Both talked and rested on the beautiful stream banks. They enjoyed heaven and all its ways. The joy of heaven was awesome!

Chapter 15

Special Beauty

Wee Angel and Felicia rested with Sir William and Little Angelica. They rested and rested on the beautiful grass of heaven.

They knew in their hearts the love of the Lord for them, and they loved him so much!

In heaven's time after resting, they went to Sir William, and Wee Angel said, "We will be going back to the Lord's Holy City."

Sir William nodded, and he looked at both Wee Angel and Felicia with so much love for being with them on so many journeys. He put his head by them. They rubbed Sir William behind his ears and rubbed his forehead. They hugged his large neck as best they could!

"Oh Sir William(Revelation), you have been so mighty special to us. We can't say enough and how much we love you. Our hearts are so full of love. I don't know why I have so many tears in my eyes. "We love you so much!" Wee Angel said.

Felicia quietly said, "Wee Angel, you are so right."

Tears flowed from her eyes too! Both cried and cried, saying, "Sir William, thank you so much on all of these journeys."

Little Angelica was close and nudged Sir William saying her way how she loved him. With this, Wee Angel and Felicia quietly got on the back of Sir William. He walked to an open area where he could open his mighty wings, and soon they were back into the skies of heaven in flight towards God's Holy City.

He quietly winged onward over heaven's lands. Wee Angel and Felicia were so full of love as he flew along with Little Angelica. Streams, forests, hills, golden path, saints, angels, animals of heaven, birds of heaven under and around them.

Sometimes angels and saints with wings flew close by them with good-days, feeling the love of heaven. Sir William(Revelation) winged quietly onward, and soon more little angels flew from a distance.

It wasn't too long, and Wee Angel and Felicia knew it was their closest friends, Angel Gabriella and

Angel Daniella. Both flew right up to Wee Angel and Felicia.

"We are coming with you," said Angel Daniella.

"Yes, we are coming with you," said Angel Gabriella.

Sir William flew with several other angels. Then, Toby flew with Annie as they joined in the flight. They nodded gently to each one. It wasn't too long, and they started to see the glories of God's Holy City.

More saints on horses flew closer to them and joined in with the flight. Sometimes some with the group would slowly fly away on their own.

"I'm just happy!" Felicia said.

Wee Angel quietly nodded to her. They had so much in their hearts — this joy of heaven.

Chapter 16

The Meeting about Earth

The group was getting closer to God's Holy City. Quietly another friend Noah with Majestic flew upwards and joined in with the group. They continued to fly closer to the city. Wee Angel said to Felicia, "Sir William will be flying to the gate of the city where we were before that had the many olive trees."

Felicia nodded to her. Within time, they were there, and Sir William quietly landed on the grass with the golden path very close by them just outside the city gate.

With this, the other saints on winged horses went about their way and after they greeted Wee Angel, Felicia, Angel Gabriella, and Angel Daniella.

Soon they were quietly sitting by some fruit trees, resting, and reflecting on all that had happened to them. All the animal friends and Majestic were close by them.

We are to wait here for something special."

All of them continued to rest, yet in heaven, some of their little friends came to them. Of course, one of them was Tuddley Teddy and Golden too! With this many more hugs and Tuddley Teddy to be with them. They took the time to play with them. Soon in the distance, they saw a group of winged horses in flight. Again they knew these white-winged horses and riders were a part of the Lord's army. There were about 25 horses and riders with tremendous light surrounding them.

In an orderly fashion, they landed near them on the open grass and lined up all in a straight row. They knew two of the riders, one was David, and the other was Joshua. They left their horses, and quickly Wee Angel, Felicia, Angel Daniella, and Angel Gabriella ran toward them with joy in their hearts, giving them the biggest hugs. David and Joshua picked each one up and hugged them. David and Joshua had some tears in their eyes. They quietly walked and greeted Tuddley Teddy and the other little ones there.

Within heaven's time, angels started to move above them and alone on the sides of the golden path to the city. They were quietly singing and praising the Father. The area became very glorious with the praises and glories by these angels to God. So many feelings, the emotions flowed through each one's heart as they talked and had fellowship. Angel Gabriella and Angel Daniella flew up and sat on Sir William's back, as he was so happy to be with Tuddley, Annie, Noah, Majestic, Golden, and all his little friends. Joshua and David groomed Revelation, and gave him a big hug too! Within time, they looked up the golden road and soon saw Jesus walking with Simon Peter towards them. Soon they talked with Joshua and David.

Wee Angel, Felicia, Angel Gabriella, and Angel Daniella waited with the little ones by some trees.

Jesus, David, Joshua, and Simon Peter talked for quite a long time. Then quietly, David came and said for them to go and greet Jesus. All four walked to Jesus and gave him big hugs.

Jesus said to Wee Angel and Felicia, "I heard you had quite an experience in your trip to earth. Just know we will be handling that in our time."

Jesus said they should wait by the trees with their little friends.

He continued to talk to Joshua, David, and Simon Peter. It seemed they had a lot on their minds.

Wee Angel and Felicia rested and played with their little friends.

Chapter 17

Jesus Talking to Joshua, David, Simon Peter, and Archangels

Wee Angel and Felicia had so much on their hearts.

They took some time and walked with the little ones.

"Tuddley Teddy, we love you so much! Wee Angel and Felicia said together. "Annie, Noah, Majestic, we love you too!"

Then finally Angel Daniella, Angel Gabriella said to Felicia and Wee angel, that they should pray with their little ones.

They quietly said, "Dear Father, thank you for all the wonderful times we have had together and for all our friends. We thank you for Jesus, Joshua, David, and Simon Peter. We thank you, and we love you."

They continued to pray for the earth and knew that Jesus would know what to be done in its time. They greeted and spent more time with the little ones. Soon more heavenly angels flew from God's Holy City with more glories in the skies because of the angels.

Finally, beautiful praises filled the heavenly skies, as Wee Angel and Felicia said to the others, "It's like the Lord knew we needed that!"

They looked and listened to the beautiful praises. All of their hearts were so stirred with love. The moment was special. Beautiful hedges with the beautiful olive trees in the area. Sir William walked close by them and nodded his head. He loved them so much, put his head by them as they rubbed him behind the ears and groomed him. He had a tear in his eye. Sir William was happy to be with them. Tuddley Teddy came, and he had a tear in his eye. Then Noah, Little Angelica, Toby, Annie, Majestic, Golden as they even had some tears in their eyes.

Angel Gabriella and Angel Daniella said, "Oh! How beautiful!"

Angel Gabriella said, "Wee Angel and Felicia, how we love you both so much! We are always so happy to be with you. We talk about that when we are away from you! We have had so much joy in being with you."

Now all of them had tears in their eyes. They have had so many beautiful times already in heaven, and they knew there would be many more, as the tears of joy continued to flow from their eyes.

Tuddley Teddy and Annie stood close by them, and they seemingly still had tears in their eyes. Oh, the love was strong as they talked, prayed, thanked the Lord on these heavenly lands.

The angels quietly sang praises of joy to the Father.

Some with instruments played, the sounds were awesome, and the moment was special! The glories above God's Holy City seemingly even got brighter with all that was happening there.

Angel Gabriella said, "Thank you again for being our friends."

They knew much was on the mind of Jesus. They knew that! They knew on earth times were not the best. They knew that! They stood and continued to praise the Lord in their own special way. More angels flew into the skies.

Archangel Micah soon came flying and joined Jesus. Then Archangel Michael arrived and joined Jesus. They talked on! More power of God was present as the light was so over-whelming to all of them.

Chapter 18

Jesus, Wee Angel, Felicia, Angel Daniella and Angel Gabriella

The angels continued to sing glories and praise the Lord. The discussion of Jesus continued with David, Joshua, Simon Peter, Archangel Micah, and Archangel Michael. Then in the distance, another grouping of white-winged horses flew closer to everyone.

Soon one by one landed on the grass near the other horse and riders. Another 30 to 40 white-winged horses. The leader of the white-winged horses was in this group, and he walked over to the meeting.

Wee Angel said, "No matter what, it must be something very important, or at least it sure looks that way!"

All of them remembered the last time when Jesus had a special talk with David, Joshua, and the leader.

Angel Daniella and Angel Gabriella were grooming Sir William. Wee Angel and Felicia watched and gave the others attention too. The angels continued to sing glories to the Father, and play the instruments.

The discussion went on!

The heavens rang with glory! Olive trees glowed as always, the streams that flowed so close by them were so beautiful with hedges of flowers and groupings of flowers.

The meeting went on for quite some time, even heavenly time, as Jesus continued to talk and meet with them. Wee Angel, Felicia, and the others waited and kept up the beauty of heaven's ways as they were joyful, with hearts that were so full of joy.

Angel Daniella and Angel Gabriella shared how much love they had in being with Wee Angel and Felicia, the little ones, and Sir William.

They were so happy to be again together for this moment of friendship just outside God's Holy City. The joy of the angels that continued to praise quietly was awesome. The heavens rang with glory as God's Holy City was so radiant everywhere.

Then within heaven's time, Jesus ended the meeting. He bid good-days to everyone. David and Joshua walked over to Wee Angel, Felicia, Angel Daniella, and Angel Gabriella picked up and hugged each one.

Soon Jesus slowly walked over to them, smiled, greeted the little ones. The angels continued to sing, many praises to the Father. Jesus looked at all of them with so much love in his eyes. He knew they had been through a lot, and his love was so awesome.

He had a couple of tears in his eyes as he continued to greet them.

Then he said, "Come with me. Come with me to the City."

They quietly said their good-days to Sir William(Revelation), Tuddley Teddy, and the others. Jesus took some time and hugged Revelation. A beautiful sight to see Jesus and Revelation together!

Then Jesus started to walk up the golden path as the angels above continued to sing praises. Jesus took hold of Wee Angel's hand to his left and Felicia with his right hand. Angel Gabriella to the left side of Wee Angel and Angel Daniella to the right side of Felicia.

They walked slowly, as Jesus didn't say much! They continued to walk on back into God's Holy City. This love of heaven was real, and the journeys had been many for Wee Angel and Felicia. Sir William and the others watched with heavenly joy in their hearts. Many had been on a lot of journeys themselves.

The animals watched as they walked further away from them. A scene of beauty, a scene of love as heaven was so real, and life was beautiful, quiet yet majestic as angels, everything there praised the Father. Jesus told them to look around, and they did!

With this, Wee Angel, Angel Daniella, Angel Gabriella, and Felicia saw the little ones all standing so closely watching them.

Jesus said, "You see how they wait and watch for you to come back to them. You see, they miss you! Now you see how I see in missing others that aren't a part of heaven. How I wait for them."

Now they had many tears in their eyes, for they knew what Jesus spoke about to them. They continued to look at their friends as they stood and watched them.

Then Wee Angel and the others waved, put their hands to their lips, and gave a little kiss into the air with their hands.

"We love you!" They said together.

"We love you!" they said again.

Jesus smiled!

Then they turned and walked further up the golden road, talking with Jesus. Joy was in their hearts as Jesus walked, holding Wee Angel's and Felicia's hands, with Angel Gabriella, and Angel Daniella holding their hands. They walked on into God's Holy City.

From the Author

As the author, I never thought the Lord would go to this territory of writing!

All I know that when I felt I was to write more, I should be ready for powerful writing!

All the writing was done around 1 to 4 am! I got up with paper and a pen. A little unsure, but as I sat down, the writing thoughts went extremely quick. I couldn't seem to write as fast as the words and scenes appeared!

After the first night of writing, I knew the Lord wanted books 6 and 7 written. Both manuscripts were written in about 18 days. I was exhausted!

Again I feel so strong, "Unless the Days be Shortened! "Enjoy Book 6 of this unique, one of a kind series.

DANIEL

Daniel Leske

Daniel Leske is available for speaking engagements and public appearances. For more information contact:

Daniel Leske
C/O Advantage Books
P.O. Box 160847
Altamonte Springs, FL 32716

info@ advbooks.com

Daniel has also published *The Joy of Heaven 1, 2, 3, 4, and 5* all available from *Advantage Books*

To purchase additional copies of this book or other books published by *Advantage Books* call our order number at:

407-788-3110 (Book Orders Only)

or visit our bookstore website at: www.advbookstore.com

We are planning to have some children's products of the characters from *The Joy of Heaven 1, 2, 3, 4 and 5*. They would be stuffed animal toys, teddy bears, figurines, possibly dolls and other products. For more information:

www.thejoyofheaven.com

Facebook: Daniel Leske / Author

Longwood, Florida, USA
"we bring dreams to life"™
www.advbookstore.com

www.ingramcontent.com/pod-product-compliance
Lightning Source LLC
LaVergne TN
LVHW081326060426
835511LV00011B/1881